Depression Glass
Dinnerware Accessories

Doris Yeske

4880 Lower Valley Road, Atglen, PA 19310 USA

Dedication

As requested by my daughter, Sharon, I dedicate this book to my husband, James, posthumously, who enjoyed the collection of this memorable glassware.

With her frequent visits to our house, Sharon has acquired an avid interest in Depression glass, Elegant glass, and other glassware. She is now pursuing the family tradition of collecting and preserving this historical glassware.

Published by Schiffer Publishing Ltd.
4880 Lower Valley Road
Atglen, PA 19310
Phone: (610) 593-1777; Fax: (610) 593-2002
E-mail: Info@schifferbooks.com

For the largest selection of fine reference books on this and related subjects, please visit our web site at **www.schifferbooks.com**
We are always looking for people to write books on new and related subjects. If you have an idea for a book please contact us at the above address.

This book may be purchased from the publisher.
Include $3.95 for shipping.
Please try your bookstore first.
You may write for a free catalog.

In Europe, Schiffer books are distributed by
Bushwood Books
6 Marksbury Ave.
Kew Gardens
Surrey TW9 4JF England
Phone: 44 (0) 20 8392-8585; Fax: 44 (0) 20 8392-9876
E-mail: info@bushwoodbooks.co.uk
Free postage in the U.K., Europe; air mail at cost.

Designed by Mark David Bowyer
Type set in Aldine 721 BT

ISBN: 0-7643-2286-9
Printed in China
1 2 3 4

Contents

Acknowledgments

My deepest gratitude to the members of the antique club "Tickled by Time" and other friends for their enthusiasm, support, and contribution of glassware for this book.

These include Barbara Dalton, Anita Tanke, Mary Powell, Marsha Gartner, Lorraine Terry, Kay Lawnicke, and Irene Schieck of La Crosse, Wisconsin; Jean Wolfe, Marlene McCabe, Lyle Fokken, and Carmen Deeth of Onalaska, Wisconsin; Sandy Jack, Sandy Goetzman, and Marion Fried of West Salem, Wisconsin; Kelly Saterbak of Coon Valley, Wisconsin; Ruth Ann Holm of Sparta, Wisconsin; Marilyn Meyer of Holmen, Wisconsin; and Linda Rhodes of La Crescent, Minnesota.

As I demonstrated these dinnerware accessories at our club meeting and banquet, the club members were so impressed with the variety and how each piece adapted to the serving needs. Discussing and displaying them, they all agreed that more emphasis should be placed on these all-purpose accessories. The information they provided and their willingness to loan me pieces to photograph has been overwhelming. Without their tremendous support, this book would not be possible.

A special thank you to my daughter, Karen, and son-in-law, Marc Imhof, for loaning me some very special glassware to use in the book.

Also, a special thank you to my daughter, Sharon Frenna, of Houston, Texas, and to Lyle Fokken, of Onalaska, Wisconsin, for their extraordinary time-consuming task of preparing the manuscript.

I am deeply indebted to my photographers, Steve Noffke, of West Salem, Wisconsin, and Doug Congdon-Martin, of Atglen, Pennsylvania, who came into the homes to photograph the glassware. In their available hours, they assisted me in the selection and artistic arrangement of the glassware for this book. Thanks to their technical expertise and experience, the pictures are exquisite.

Finally, thanks to my friend Michael Merola, of La Crosse, Wisconsin, for his helpful suggestions and ideas regarding this book. As he so aptly noted, "This glassware will always remain popular—yesterday, today, and tomorrow."

Preface

The numerous pieces in the dinnerware sets produced in Depression glass and other glassware have always amazed me.

While glancing through my collection, searching through shops, and identifying usage of the pieces, I became more aware of the beauty, variety, and functionality of these accessories.

With so little information on this, I felt the need to explore and expand on these pieces by writing a book. Mentioning this to my publisher, he fully agreed that this would be a good topic. This book, therefore, focuses on the variety, descriptions, and the proper usage of these dinnerware accessories. The coordinated table settings of the 1930s and beyond can be just as popular today.

Introduction

Engaged in more entertaining recently, I discovered the variety of the unique and versatile dinnerware accessories of the Depression era and beyond. Prior to this, it appeared that I would just display and use them at random.

I realized I wasn't fully aware of the specific pieces with the beauty, style, and functionality that comprised the table settings. This sparked my attention and I began to use various ones for my luncheons, dinners, casual parties, and especially for festive entertaining. My guests were completely enthralled and eager to explore what they had, and to search for them to use as well.

As a result, I, too, wanted to become more familiar with how these accessories, produced specifically for the needs and eating habits of that particular time in history, could be used today.

My goal in writing this book was to expand and focus on these accessories and to categorize them. Included are numerous pictures, descriptions, and specific uses, along with current prices. I'm hoping this book will provide the incentive for all collectors and non-collectors to become familiar with, appreciate, and use these dinnerware accessories to glamorize their own dinners, thus retaining the gracious style of an earlier era.

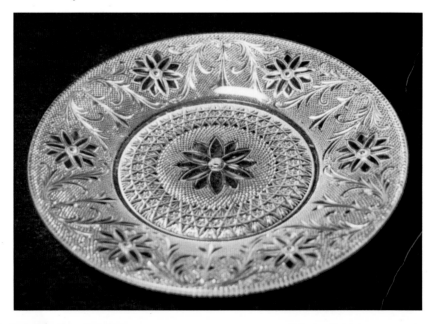

Price Guide

Prices listed here are for glass items in mint condition, meaning no chips, cracks, flakes, or extreme wear marks. If present, these will definitely affect the price by 50 percent or more. Prices on rare items may be reduced by 25 percent and probably more depending upon the amount of damage done. These prices are only a guide due to regional differences which determine the supply and demand. The prices listed here are the prices found in antique shops, shows, flea markets, and from various dealers in the Midwest. Dealers have a tremendous impact upon the determination of the prices.

Chapter One

Centerpieces
for Table Settings

The centerpiece is the focal point that graces a dinner table. What is more eye-catching than an attractive vase of freshly cut or artificial flowers?

Candlesticks, a favorite of mine, come in various shapes and brilliant colors and provide much glamour along with a little romance. They provide a perfect accent for the holidays.

A decorative handled tray, an elegant bowl, and even a tidbit would also be a useful and attractive centerpiece. Creativity is the key for table centerpieces.

Slone Glass Co., Green Spring, West Virginia. Vase, cranberry flash, cut to clear, and beautifully decorated in a floral light cranberry color. An attractive centerpiece. $25.

Hobnail, Fenton Art Glass Co. A popular white color with distinctive raised hobs. Vase, 12" swung, footed. A floral centerpiece. $28.

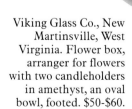

Viking Glass Co., New Martinsville, West Virginia. Flower box, arranger for flowers with two candleholders in amethyst, an oval bowl, footed. $50-$60.

Cambridge Glass Co., Cambridge, Ohio. Candle set, Cambridge Arms with peg vases, bobeches, and prisms. An elaborate candelabrum. $75-$80.

Cambridge Glass Co., Cambridge, Ohio. Candle set, Cambridge Arms, an elegant set with flowers floats on a candleholder. $50.

Fostoria Glass Co. Trojan etched pattern made from 1929-1944. Candlestick #2395 ½, scroll. 5", topaz color. $100-$125 (pair).

Paden City Glass Co., Paden City, West Virginia. #221 Maya two-light candlesticks, fan shaped with a light floral cutting on the base. $50-$60 (pair).

New Martinsville-Viking Glass Co., New Martinsville, West Virginia. Swan set, an oval swan 12-1/2" in emerald green with a crystal neck, very graceful. $75-$85. Swan candleholders, "Sweethearts" shape, 5". $30-$35 each.

Lancaster Glass Co., Jubilee cut pattern of the early 1930s. The elegant pattern is elaborately decorated with an exquisite floral and leaf design with twelve petals with an open design center. Pink, $185 (pair). Topaz, $190 (pair).

Diamond Glass Company, Indiana, Pennsylvania. Lovely console set with two baluster candlesticks, matching bowl, and amethyst stand. Light green color with iridescent finish from the Rainbow Lustre lines made in 1922-1923. $150-$200 (set).

U.S. Glass / Tiffin, 1920s-1930s. #300 Candlesticks and console bowl set. Rare color called Jasper. $125-$150.

Lancaster Glass Co., Jubilee, early 1930s. An elegant cut pattern elaborately decorated with an exquisite floral and leaf design defined by twelve petal flowers with open centers. $435 (set).

Paden City Glass Co., Paden City, West Virginia. Five-piece water set includes the #180 wide optic pitcher and #2108 tumblers in green. Acid etched and gold encrusted floral band around each piece. $250-$300.

Hocking Glass Co., Mayfair "Open Rose," 1931-1937. Pattern consists of a center circle of roses with widely spaced lines, a border of roses, and a scalloped edge. Deep fruit bowl, 12", blue, rare. $110.

Imperial Glass Co., Bellaire, Ohio. 1920s-1950s. This company is known for its large line of colors and specially designed products. 12" Bowl, fruit or muffin; elegantly designed footed boat shaped with turned up sides. $40-$45.

Dugan Glass Co., Indiana, Pennsylvania. Ruffled edge pink bowl in the Cherry pattern. Three ball shaped feet on the underside. $30-$40.

A.H. Heisey & Co., Newark, Ohio. Plantation #1567 blank. A very popular pattern at the present time in spite of the high prices. Crystal with pineapples and a beautifully crimped rim. 13" fruit or flower bowl. $110.

Jeannette Glass Company. Swirl, "Petal Swirl," 1937-1938. Pattern has a motif of concentric ribbed circles and an outer rim of swirled ribs on the border. Bowl, 10", footed, closed handles. $35.

Lancaster Glass Co., Jubilee pattern, early 1930s. An elegant cut pattern elaborately decorated with an exquisite floral and leaf design defined by twelve petal flowers with open centers. Two-piece Cheese & Cracker set. $300 (rare).

Fenton Art Glass Co. Diamond Lace pattern, 1948-1954. Epergne, large, blue opalescent with three "Jack in the Pulpit" shaped horns. $250.

Fostoria Glass Company. Epergne #2723/364, consisting of one crystal 10" bowl and three amethyst removable trumpet shaped vases. Only made in 1959 and hardest to find in the amethyst color. $175.

Chapter Two

The Adorning Vases

Many of the Depression glass patterns both earlier and later featured a variety of vases ranging from small to large. The average size is 6" to 11-1/4" inches, while the shapes range from fan, elliptical, cupped, flared, straight, bulbous with flat rim, round, square, ribbed flip with cover, and straw vase. More decorative ones were beaded, ruffled, rimmed, three-legged, parfait, two handled, rocket bud, cone shaped, crimped ball ivy, frosted, and the unique cornucopia. Some patterns had more than one vase. All of them are attractive, very useful, and fun to display. For decorating with seasonal colors, they are ideal.

So attractive in the 1920s to the 30s, as well as during the 1940s to the 60s, vases are the perfect accessories for all dinnerware settings. Not only were they popular then they are fashionable today in elegant crystal.

Candlewick, Imperial Glass Co., 1936-1984. This is elegant crystal glassware with outstanding and unique beaded edges. Vase, 6", fan shape. $45.

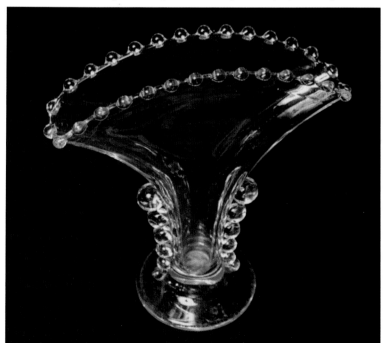

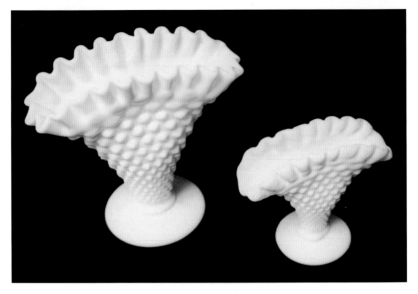

Hobnail, Fenton Art Glass Co. A very popular variety of the white glassware with raised knobs made in a wide variety of shapes. Vase, 6-1/4", fan shape, $24. Vase, 4", fan shape, $15.

Ovide, Hazel Atlas Glass Co., 1930-1935. An unusually shaped oval-like vase with a crimped top, frosted finish, and black drizzled enamel decoration. Vase, $10.

Yorktown, Federal
Glass Co., 1950s.
Pattern consists of
rows of rounded corner
rectangular blocks.
Vase, 8". Yellow, $20;
Crystal, $17.

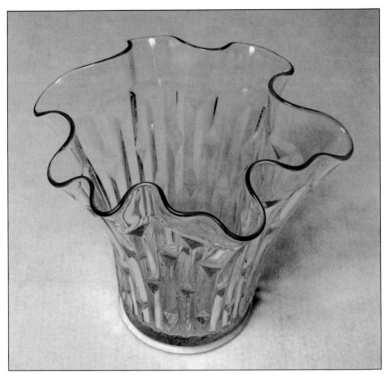

Frances, Line #2010, Central Glass Works, later 1920s. An occasional piece produced in a delicate pink with diamonds over vertical ribs. Pulled and crimped top. Vase, 7-3/4". $95-$125 (not common).

Pineapple Vase, Anchor Hocking Glass Co., 1950s-1960s. Pineapple shaped vase with block pattern on the base and flared crimped rim. Pink, $35; Crystal, $15.

American "Whitehall," Indiana Glass Co. (1986 or earlier). An elegant pattern consisting of brilliant cubes throughout the glassware. Vase, $15.

Iris, "Iris and Herringbone," Jeannette Glass Co., 1928-1932, 1950-1970. Very attractive with the unusual large spray of iris with its blade like leaves creating a bouquet effect. Vase, 9". Crystal, $30; Iridescent, $20.

Harp, Jeannette Glass Co.,
1954-1957. A very beautiful
pattern with a musical name,
featuring a harp or lyre in a
dainty allover beading, even
on the bottom. Vase, 7-1/2".
$30.

Jubilee, cutting #1200,
Lancaster Glass Co., early
1930s. An elegant cut pattern
elaborately decorated with an
exquisite floral and leaf design
defined by twelve petal flowers
with open centers. Pink bud
vase, 10". $600.

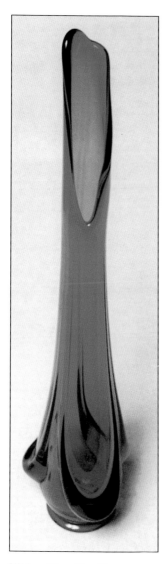

Viking Glass Co., New Martinsville, West Virginia. This company made quality pieces in various shapes and colors. Bud vase, blue, narrow top with a round and swirled bottom. $20.

Kemple Glass Works, Kenova, West Virginia. Tall vase with rainbow pattern design and a slightly crimped edge. $15.

Soreno, Fire King, Anchor Hocking Glass
Co., 1966. This pattern contains a continuous rippled scroll design in a continuing
circle. Many people refer to this as Green
Bark. $10 each.

Capri, Hazel Ware division of
Continental Can, 1960-1970. This
pattern refers to the blue color so
popular in the 1960s. "Dots" is
one of the Capri designs. Vase, 8",
blue "Dots." $20.

Hobnail, Fenton Art Glass
Co. Swung footed vase, 12".
Pure white color, $28.

Swirl "Petal Swirl," Jeannette Glass Co., 1937-1938. Pattern has a motif of concentric ribbed circles and an outer rim of swirled ribs on the border. Left: Vase, 6-1/2" footed. Right: Vase, 8-1/2" footed. $28-$30 each.

Hobnail, Fenton Art Glass Co. Pattern has a snow white color with numerous hobs in different crimped and scalloped shapes. Vase, 6" scalloped top, $20. Vases, 3-3/4" crimped top, $10 each..

Cobalt Blue, produced by several companies in
the 1920s and 30s in limited quantities.
Left to right: ruffled vase, $25; etched bud
vase, $20; vase with narrow optic, $15.

Moonstone, Hocking Glass Co.,
1941-1946. Very attractive with
opalescent crystal hobnails with
crimped and plain rims giving a
bluish effect. Vase, 5-1/2". $24.

Pineapple Vase, Anchor Hocking Glass Co. 1950s-1960s. Pineapple shaped vase with block pattern on the base and flared rim. Forest Green, $35.

Ring, "Banded Rings," Hocking Glass Co. Line #300, 1927-1932. A popular pattern of crystal decorated with various colors of horizontal ribbed bands molded in a circle design. Vase, 8" iridescent, $18. Vase, 8" decorated, $40.

Warwick #1428, A.H. Heisey & Co., Newark, Ohio, 1933-1957. Also referred to as Horn of Plenty. Very elegant glassware with respect to quality, composition, and design. Vases, 9" cornucopia, $50 each.

Forest Green and Royal Ruby, Anchor Hocking, 1950s-1967 (green), 1939- 1960s (red). Rich solid colors extremely popular for the holidays. Vases, 6-3/8", red and green, "Coolidge," $9-$10. Vase (center), 9" "Hoover," $18-$20 (ideal flower vase).

L. E. Smith Co., 1920s-1934. A great distributor of the black
glassware in striking designs and good quality. Vase, 8" crimped
top, two handled with a sterling floral design. $45-$50.

MacBeth-Evans Glass Co., Charleroi, Pennsylvania. This is an incredible topaz vase with hand-applied handles and a wide optic. The sides are cut with a flower and leaf pattern certainly done by either the Lancaster or Standard divisions of Hocking Glass. $500.

Chapter Three

Center Handled
Trays and Bowls

These numerous and fanciful trays, often called sandwich servers, were something of a phenomenon produced in the 1920s, 30s, and beyond. All of these items in various colors, so unique with the special effects in the dinnerware lines, were quite representative of the Depression era.

They adapted, too, for other eating needs, such as serving small sandwiches, petit fleurs, cookies, candies, and relishes.

As decorations, they are wonderful for flowers. For holiday decorating, they can be used to hold Christmas ornaments, Easter eggs, miniature pumpkins, and other objects that provide an attractive centerpiece for the table.

Trojan, Fostoria Glass Co., 1929-1944.
Center handled tray #2375. $95.

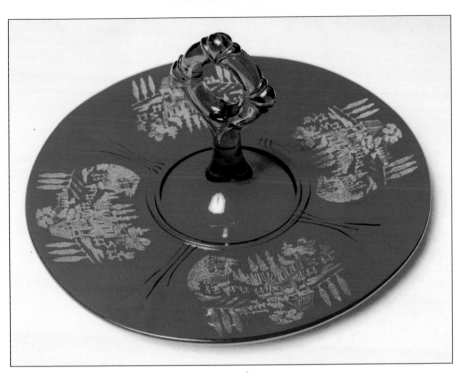

Lucy, Paden City Glass Co., Paden City, West Virginia.
#895 Ruby center handled tray with acid etched and gold
encrusted Oriental Garden pattern. $165-$180.

Tea Room, Indiana Glass Co., 1926-1931. Pink center handled
tray with a very art deco style of stepped squares. The pattern
has many points on the underside that chip easily so it is very
difficult to find in excellent condition. $150.

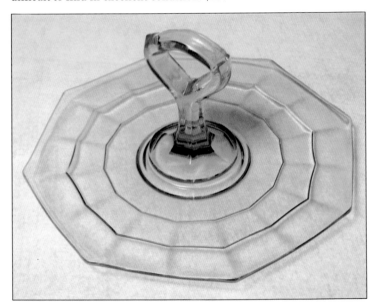

Cambridge Glass Co. Cobalt blue, center handled tray with etched and gold encrusted pattern #707. Striking contrast with the elegant gold on the dark blue glass. $65.

Teardrop, Indiana Glass Co., Dunkirk, Indiana. Center handled tray, brilliant crystal in a teardrop effect design, surrounded by a floral cut band, scalloped edge with a sturdy handle. $25.

"Charade" pattern produced in the 1920s and 1930s. Tray, center handled server, 10" black glass with slightly pointed and ruffled edging. $42.

Hobnail, Fenton Art Glass Co., 1943-present. A very attractive white glass (milk glass) with distinctive hobs and designed with crimping, ruffled, and flared edging. Tray, 7-3/4", chrome handle (center) with cream and sugar. $50-$55.

Ring, "Banded Rings," Line #300, Hocking Glass Co., 1927-1932.
A popular pattern of crystal with horizontal ribbed bands molded
in a circle design. Center handled server in undecorated crystal,
$18. With colored bands, $30.

Indiana Glass Co., 1930s-1940s. Center handled refreshment tray made to hold six lemonade tumblers. A very unique and sturdy item whose function remains useful to the present day. $18.

Petalware, MacBeth-Evans Glass Company. A lovely pattern that was very popular and made for over twenty years beginning in the early 1930s. Monax opal color with outward stretched rounded ribs on the underside. These servers were made in many styles. $20.

Westmoreland Glass Co., Grapeville, Pennsylvania. Crystal #1849 Butterball center handled tray. A unique specialty item produced with an enameled color bottom and gold encrusted "hammered" border. Small 6" size used to hold butter. $35.

Diamond, Federal Glass Co., 1930-1936. Center handled tidbit in a diamond point design with distinct pointed edges, grayish blue color. $10-$12.

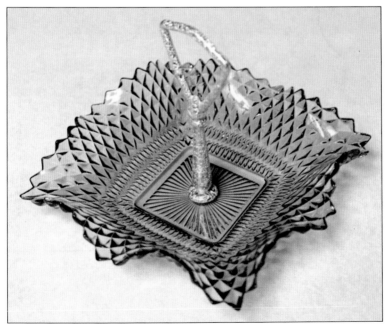

Bonbons, produced in the 1930s, were very popular in the colors of pink, green, amber, and black. Left to right: Imperial Glass, heart handled with indentations and points, $20; Hocking Glass, mint dish with center handle, rayed design, curved edges, $22; Fostoria, two handled lemon dish in amber, $15.

Jubilee, Lancaster Glass Co. Delicate pink center handled tray. Jubilee is the name of the floral cutting that is an exquisite floral and leaf design with twelve petals with an open design center. $220.

Fostoria Glass Company. Green center handled 11" tray #2287, 1929-1944; Rose cutting possibly done by Lotus Decorating Co. $40.

Crow's Foot, Paden City Glass Co., Paden City, West Virginia. Crystal center handled tray with beautiful sterling silver swan decoration done by Rockwell. The underside center area is frosted to make the swans appear to be floating on water. Teardrops in a row design on the underside. $75-$100.

Yummy, Standard Glass Manufacturing Co, Lancaster Ohio. These 11" center handled trays were made at Lancaster Glass Company and then cut by Standard. Lancaster and Standard were both divisions of Hocking Glass at the time. They have the same twelve petal flowers with open center that the Lancaster Jubilee pattern has and are often combined with that pattern. Topaz , $210. Pink, $195.

Dunbar Flint Glass Corp, Dunbar, West Virginia. This is the tray from the #1247 Servette Set that came with four matching tumblers in the late 1920s. Seen in pink, green, and crystal. $25.

Tea Room, Indiana Glass Co. 1926-1931. An early pattern made for restaurants and soda fountains. Resembles decorative style of the 1920s and 30s, extreme in style. Heavy pressed, geometric and flashy shapes. Center ringed handle tray with cream and sugar. $90-$100.

Jubilee, Lancaster Glass Co. Cut pattern of the early 1930s. The elegant pattern elaborately decorated with an exquisite floral and leaf design with twelve petals with an open design center. Center handled tray with cream and sugar. Topaz, $180. Pink, $150.

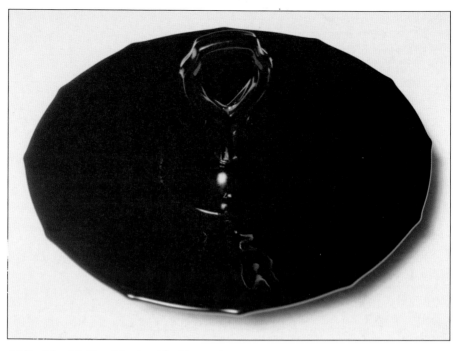

Addie, Line 34, New Martinsville Glass Mfg Co. 12-pointed
center handled tray in ebony. This tray can be found in various
colors and is part of a full table service made in the 1930s. $35.

Bonbon, produced in the 1930s, very popular in the color pink.
Center handled with ray design and curved edges for mints. $22.

Trudy, cut #88, Standard Glass Mfg. Co. Wonderful center handled tray holding a cream and sugar. The set was likely made at Lancaster Glass Company and then cut by Standard. Lancaster and Standard were both divisions of Hocking Glass at the time. The cutting is a flower much like the Jubilee flower with the addition of a swagged lattice on the top edge. $75.

L.E. Smith / Greensburg Glass. #200 center handled bonbon in solid black. Smith acquired Greensburg in the same period of production and they produced an assortment of bowls, trays, candlesticks, and ashtrays. $20.

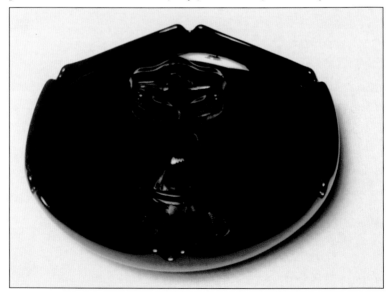

Gothic Garden, Paden City Glass Co. Yellow topaz #411
center handled tray with etching on the underside
featuring a flower filled urn with birds on each side. $75.

Chapter Four

Traditional
Tidbit Servers

These sets, today called party servers, were also something of a phenomenon in the 1940s, 50s, and early 60s. They have currently become more and more popular and are seen frequently in restaurants featuring candies and various snacks and used for displaying advertising cards. Today, they could be called hors d'oeuvres servers.

A tidbit is a two or three layer piece with a metal upright handle. Most consist of the traditional two or three bowls or plates that are stacked and set in with a center metal rod. Some have a white or tan wooden post.

Sandwich, Anchor Hocking Glass Co., 1939, 1964-1979.
Pattern has an allover stippling spaced around flowers, foliage, and scroll motifs in an elaborate arrangement. Tidbit, $25.

They were produced by enterprising individuals for years. Many have been constructed recently by using older hardware and drilling into the regular plates. These pieces were made to be taken apart so the chrome can be polished with the proper product and the glass can be washed.

I use mine for special events, for serving mints, candies, crackers, cheese slices, and an assortment of snacks. They can actually be space savers compared to using individual dishes. They also serve another purpose: a place for storing clips, cards, and handy items that you use daily.

Convenience and versatility describe these tidbit servers, which make ideal centerpieces for a dinner table.

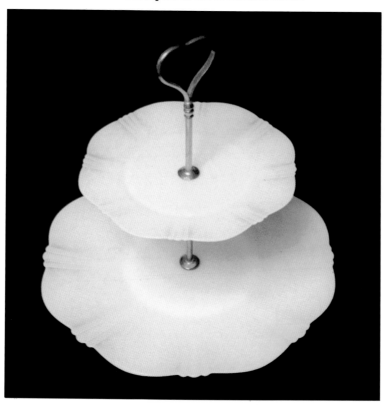

American Sweetheart, MacBeth-Evans Glass Co., 1931-1936. A delicate pattern with a neat arrangement consisting of a center motif of festoons, ribbons, and scrolls with smaller ones surrounding the scalloped rim with short lines. Tidbit, 2 tier, 8" and 12" plates, Monax. $60.

Hazel Atlas Glass Co., 1930-1936. A unique
center handled tidbit in a diamond point
design with an angle design handle. $20.

Anniversary, Jeannette Glass Co., 1947-1949, 1960s-1970s.
Pattern consists of numerous vertical ribs with open clear spaces
at the top of many pieces. Tidbit, berry and fruit bowls. $14.

Left:
Silver Crest, Fenton Art Glass Co., 1943-present. A very
attractive white glass (milk glass) with edging encompass-
ing crystal ruffled and crimped edges. Left to right:
Tidbit, 2 tier (#7296 luncheon/dessert plates), $50;
Tidbit, 2 tier (#7294 luncheon/dinner plates), $65.

Sandwich, Indiana Glass Co., 1920s-1980s. This pattern has an allover stippling spaced around flowers, foliage, and scroll motifs. Tidbit, (6" bowl, 10" plate). $25.

Clover Blossom, Federal Glass Co., 1950s. Gray and raspberry colored clover pattern on white milk glass. Tidbit, (berry bowl / dinner plate). $20.

The deep circular pressed diamond pattern on this set sparkles in the sunlight. Clear edges are slightly cupped and very practical. $20.

Petal pattern #2829, Federal Glass Co. Pattern characterized by various petal designs in a stylized manner, with a sunburst in the center. Tidbit, (set of three bowls). $15.

Petal pattern #2829, Federal Glass Co. Pattern characterized by various petal designs in a stylized manner, with a sunburst in the center. Tidbit, (set of three plates). $15.

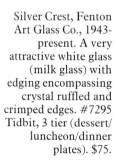

Silver Crest, Fenton Art Glass Co., 1943-present. A very attractive white glass (milk glass) with edging encompassing crystal ruffled and crimped edges. #7295 Tidbit, 3 tier (dessert/luncheon/dinner plates). $75.

Chapter Five

Serva-Snack Sets
Make a Comeback

These sets in various shapes and colors were something of another phenomenon in the 1940s, 50s, and 60s. What amazes me is how many of the popular patterns feature them.

In my travels to antique shops, flea markets, and garage sales, I've seen set after set. Picking up some of these sets, I've put them to good usage for quick entertaining. My family also enjoys using them for light snacks and desserts.

The sets come in different shapes, such as oblong, fan, round, square with edges and handles. Some are more decorated, with scalloped and flared edges. Each of the plates has a specific cup rest, i.e., an indentation fitting the cup.

These items were sold in sets of four and are usually found in the original boxes, which makes them more interesting and descriptive.

After using the fan Serva-Snack set with the Royal Ruby and Forrest Green cups, my guests were so impressed that they began to search for their own sets to use with snacks. Again, these are very convenient for quick entertaining.

Blue Mosaic, Fire King, Anchor Hocking Glass Corp., 1966 to late 1969. An attractive and sturdy set with a solid blue cup. Tray, white with little blue squares that constitute a mosaic look. Snack Set, cup 7-1/2 oz., $4; oval tray, 10" x 7-1/2", $6; 8 piece complete set, $40.

Early American Prescut, Anchor Hocking Glass Corp., 1960-1999. This is an attractive pattern in pressed glass with the plate having the distinct star deeply cut. Snack set, cup 6 oz. (no star), $2.50; plate 10", $10; 8 piece complete set, $55.

Anchor Hocking, Lancaster, Ohio. Serva-Snack set. A very unique style, with leaf pattern in plate and cup. 8 piece complete set, $25-$30.

Indiana Glass Co., Dunkirk, Indiana. Snack Set, an attractive dark green round plate with a circular design throughout, a sunburst center, and a curved circular rim. 8 piece complete set, $20-$25.

Indiana Glass Co., Dunkirk, Indiana. Snack Set, a unique triangular style in sparkling crystal with the popular snowflake design. 8 piece complete set, $20.

Federal Glass Co., Columbus, Ohio. 1920-1930s; produced again in the 1970s. A popular set in an oval shape in white glass and floral design. 8 piece complete set, mint in box, $20-$30.

Indiana Glass Co., Dunkirk, Indiana. Snack Set, a unique green floral checkered design with solid green cups. Triangular shaped. 8 piece complete set, $20.

Teardrop, Hazel Atlas Glass Division of Continental Can Company, Wheeling, West Virginia. Informal Snack Set, a crystal clear plate in a teardrop effect design with a clear cup. 8 piece complete set, $20.

Orchard Crystal, by Hazel Atlas. A wonderful apple shaped plate using a cup from the Ovide line of the early 1950s. Platonite fired on colors over white glass. Also came in colors of gray and green. 8 piece complete set, $30.

Anchor Hocking Glass Co., Lancaster, Ohio. Serva-Snack set in a fan shape, beautifully decorated in a floral, raised dots, and a scalloped edge. Very festive used with a red or green cup. Set, $13.

Soreno / Fire King, Hocking Glass Co., 1966. Pattern has a continuous rippled scroll design in a continuing circle. 8 piece complete set, $40.

Anchor Hocking Glass Co., Lancaster, Ohio. Serva-Snack set in the Grape pattern. Crystal clear plate beautifully decorated in a grape design, crimped edge, and decorated cup. 8 piece complete set, $20.

Colonial Lady, Anchor Hocking Glass Co., Lancaster, Ohio. Serva-Snack set, oblong set, trays have a circular design with added swirls and a ribbed border. 8 piece complete set, mint in box, $20.

Fire King "Fleurette," Hocking Glass Corporation, 1958-1960. White with floral decal attractive for dinnerware, tab handles, and ribbed edge. 8 piece complete set, $25.

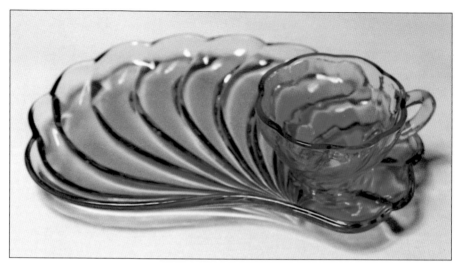

Capri, "Seashell," Hazel Ware Division of Continental Can,
1960s. Pattern consists of large "seashell" shaped swirls.
Plates are 10" fan shaped. 8 piece complete set, $56.

Orchard Crystal "Bead and Ribs" by Hazel Atlas in the 1960s.
Rectangular shaped trays with deep ribbed design. Beaded handles
and divided area to hold cup and cigarettes. 8 piece complete set, $20.

Homestead, Federal Glass Co. A very popular
crystal pattern in a circular feather design. 8 piece
complete set, mint in box, $25.

Snack Set, Jeanette Glass Co., 1936-1956. Tray, circular double flower
pattern, very unique $4; cup, Dewdrop pattern, unique with fine
panels beaded with ribbed lines, $3 (a combination).

Chapter Six

Indispensable
Relish Dishes

A table setting for dinner would be incomplete without a variety of relish dishes. In the sets produced, relish dishes were always included. Most of the patterns featured these items for dinnerware settings.

Relish dishes come in a variety of shapes, including square, round, oblong (boat like), octagonal, triangular, footed, and heart shaped. The platter type, 11-1/2" divided, is very popular. These dishes can be divided, non-divided, with handles or without handles, and range from two-part to five-part. It is interesting that some patterns from the 1950s and 60s have as many as seven parts.

Jubilee, Lancaster Glass Co., early 1930s. An elaborate pattern decorated with an exquisite floral engraving of an elegant flower and leaf design containing twelve petals with an open center. Mayonnaise, under plate, and original glass spoon. $300 each.

American, Fostoria Glass Co., Line #2056, 1915-1987. Appetizer Set includes a 10-1/2" tray and six handled inserts. America's most recognized patterns of brilliant crystal cubes throughout the glass. 7 piece complete set, $370.

Crystal oblong dish with deep pressed leaves and cut glass flowers. Brilliant, clear quality glass with a scalloped edge. $20.

Wonderful divided relish tray with spiraling ribs on the underside and a diamond pattern in the center. $15.

Candlewick Line #400, Imperial Glass Co., 1936-1984. This is elegant crystal glassware with outstanding or unique beaded edges. 10" deep divided open handled bowl. $190.

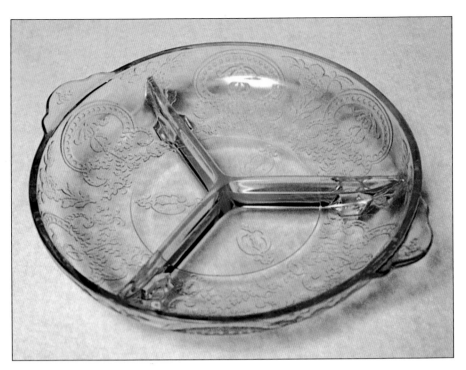

Horseshoe #612, Indiana Glass Co., 1930-1933. This pattern, especially the plate, is entirely decorated in one uninterrupted design of elaborate scroll, forming a snowflake-like pattern. Relish, 3-part, green. $40.

Waterford or Waffle, Hocking Glass Co. Relish set in Forest Green and white milk glass. Forest Green 13-3/4" tray, $25; center bowl, $6; milk glass inserts, $4 each; 7 piece complete set, $51.

Candlewick Line #400, Imperial Glass Co., 1936-1984. This is elegant crystal glassware with outstanding beaded edges. Three-piece mayonnaise consists of bowl, liner, and spoon. $55.

#1007, Indiana Glass Co. A thick heavy pattern of outward ribs and diamonds toward the center. This has a removable center dish with cover and fits on a metal lazy Susan. A wonderful item for parties. $35.

Pristine, Cambridge Glass Company. Wonderful divided mayonnaise set with liner. Very art deco in style and form. $40.

Silver Crest, Fenton Art Glass Co., 1943-present. Silver Crest, a very attractive white glass (milk glass) with edging encompassing crystal ruffled and crimped edges. Relish, heart shaped with handle. $24.

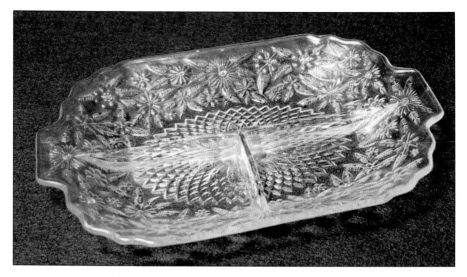

Pineapple and Floral line #618, Indiana Glass Co., 1932-1937.
A pressed pattern in the sandwich glass tradition. Center motif
is a flower surrounded by a pineapple type pressed design with
a floral border. Relish, 3-part, closed handle. $12.

Daisy line #620, Indiana Glass Co., 1930s. A pattern with the
design of daisies around the border giving it its characteristic
motif. Relish dish, 8-3/8", 3-part with three feet. $35.

Candlewick line #400, Imperial Glass Co., 1936-1984. This is elegant crystal glassware with outstanding or unique beaded edges. Bowl #55, 4-part and 4 handled, with floral cutting (scarce), $50; no cutting, $35.

Windsor / Windsor Diamond, Jeanette Glass Co., 1932-1946. A pressed pattern resembling cut crystal. Consists of a series of larger bands of diamond shaped facets emanating from a circle of radial ribs. Platter, 3-part relish. $20.

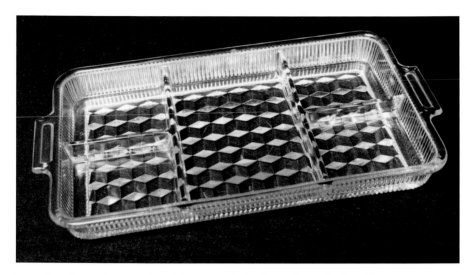

Valenti, maker unknown, circa 1920s and 30s. This relish tray is 8" x 13" and is most often found in cobalt blue in a metal holder. It has ribbed sides and a cube pattern on the underside, very much like Fostoria American. Relish in crystal, $35; cobalt, $75 (add $20 for metal tray).

Hobnail, Fenton Art Glass Co., 1943-present. A very attractive white glass (milk glass) with distinctive hobs and designed with crimping, ruffled, and flared edging. Relish, 5-1/4" x 7-1/2", 3-part #3607. $38.

Moonstone, Hocking Glass Co., 1940s. This is a very attractive pattern in crystal with opalescent hobnails and rims creating a bluish effect. Bowl, relish, 2-part, $14. Bowl, cloverleaf, 3-part, $14.

American, Fostoria Glass Co., 1915-1986. This is an elegant pattern that consists of brilliant cubes throughout the glass. Bowl, 12" relish "boat," 2-part. $25.

Mt. Pleasant or Double Shield, L.E. Smith Glass Co., 1920s and 30s. This is a pattern in black glass with alternating one and two points, making it easy to identify. Bonbon, 7" with rolled-up sides and handles. $20.

American Brilliant Period (1876-1916), cut glass pickle dish. This glass is crystal that has been cut with sharp lines and stars to reflect light brilliantly. Edges are sharp to the touch vs. the smoother pressed glass copies and there are no mold lines. $50-$65.

Oyster and Pearl, Anchor Hocking Glass Corp., 1938-1940. A very
appealing design, the rim has double ribs with pearl-like beads in between
and a scalloped edge. Bowl, 5-1/4", heart shaped jelly with handle. $15.

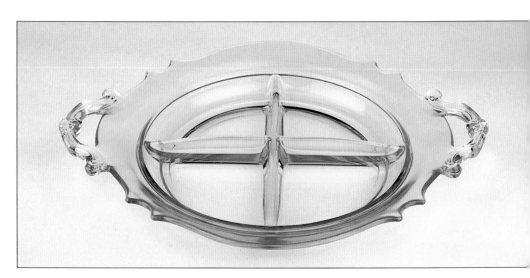

Lancaster Glass Co., Lancaster, Ohio. Four-part divided relish tray with
open handles on each side. This is the same blank that was used for Jubilee
and many other cuttings done by Lancaster and Standard. $40.

Sandwich line #41, Duncan Miller Glass Co., 1924-1955. An exquisitely
decorated pattern with scrolls, foliage, diamonds, and a beaded edge. Bowl,
5" handled 2-part nappy. $15.

Candlewick, Imperial Glass Co., 1936-1984. This is elegant
crystal glassware with outstanding and unique beaded
edges. Bowl, 8-1/2" relish, 4-part handled. $35.

Triumph line #701, Paden City Glass Co. Mayonnaise and liner etched and gold encrusted. It is octagonal in shape with a rolled over edge. $40.

Starlight, Hazel Atlas Glass Co., 1938-1940. A very unique pattern with a waffle design in the center and crossover stippled lines creating a plaid effect. Relish dish. $12.

Mt. Pleasant or Double Shield, L.E. Smith Glass Co., 1920s and 30s.
This is a pattern in black glass with alternating one and two points,
making it easy to identify. Bowl, 6" footed and handled, $20.

Pretzel, Indiana Glass Co., late 1930s-1980s. A unique
intertwined pretzel type pattern scrolled around the edges.
Dish, olive, 7" leaf shape, $8. Dish, 8-1/2" 2-handled pickle, $8.

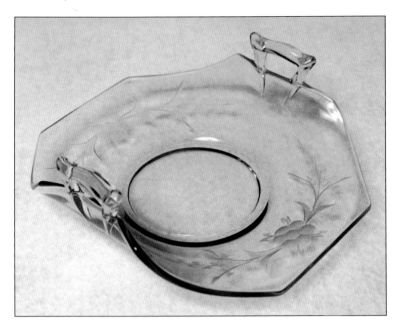

Fostoria Glass Co. Lovely turned up sides handled Bonbon in a delicate pink color. Two open handles, floral cutting engraved on the sides. $20.

Imperial, line #7255 dish with unique floral and petal cutting on its sides, 6-sided with open handles. Originally sold as a Bonbon and as a mayonnaise liner in a variety of colors. $15.

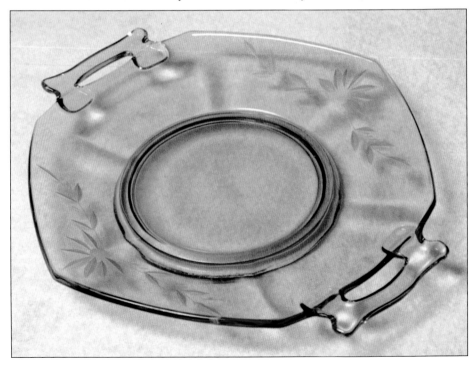

Candlewick, Imperial Glass Co., 1936-1984. This is elegant crystal glassware with outstanding or unique beaded edges. Bowl, 6" heart shaped, #51T wafer tray, $35. Marmalade, cover, and spoon, $50 (with the liner, $75).

Colony, line #412, Fostoria Glass Co., 1920s-1960s. A very distinctive pattern with swirling and slightly twisted outward stretched panels. Bowl, 5" handled, ideal relish bowl. $18.

Chapter Seven

Fascinating Candy Dishes

Candy dishes, so attractive in the various shapes and colors, were a common item produced in some of the dinnerware sets. They have become a very useful accessory today for parties, snacks, and after dinner treats.

Some of these come with covers and without covers, depending upon the style in the pattern. Unique are the ones you see on a pedestal or footed.

Candy dishes are my favorite to display and I seem to have one in every room in my house. Needless to say, they are the favorite of my grandchildren as well.

Paradise, Fostoria Glass Co., made only from 1927-1929. Lovely brocaded pattern that completely covers the outside. A floral pattern of flowers and Birds of Paradise, unique "fleur de lis" handle, 3-part divided interior. $150.

Old Quilt, line #500, Westmoreland Glass Co. Square shaped candy, footed and knob handle. Sides are paneled much like quilt squares. Milk glass, marked WG on the underside. $20.

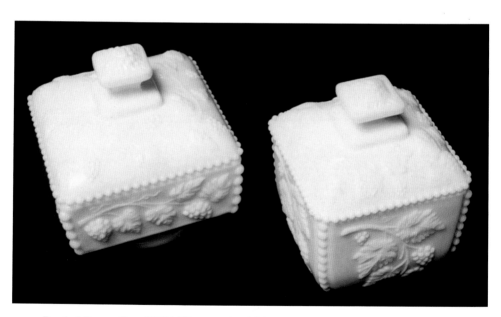

Beaded Grape, line #1884, Westmoreland Glass Co. Lovely milk glass covered candy boxes with grapes and beads on the edges and corners. Most items from this line are square in shape. Beaded Grape is a combination of two Westmoreland popular patterns, Paneled Grape and Beaded Edge. Marked WG. Footed Candy, $25. Flat, $20.

Hazel Atlas Glass Co.
Stunning, tall candy jar
with handled cover.
Pressed glass pattern of
fluted sides and cover. $15.

Molly, Imperial
Glass Co. Lovely
candy dish #717,
footed, with acorn
shaped finial, 6-
sided with a
crosshatched
cutting on the base
and cover.
$35- $45.

Trojan, Fostoria Glass Co., #2400 comport made in topaz from 1929-1936.
A very attractive etched pattern that resembles a spade with additional
scrolling around it. Makes a wonderful candy dish. $75.

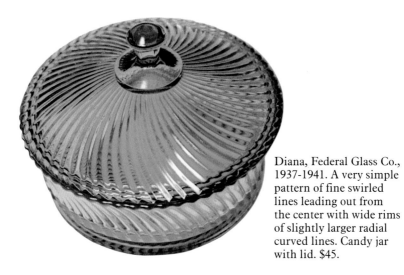

Diana, Federal Glass Co.,
1937-1941. A very simple
pattern of fine swirled
lines leading out from
the center with wide rims
of slightly larger radial
curved lines. Candy jar
with lid. $45.

Wedding Bowl, Westmoreland Glass Co., 1950s. Wedding Bowl (Line #1874) is a copy of a very old 1890s pressed glass pattern called Crystal Wedding. It has a unique square shape with indented edges. Marketed strongly as a gift item and made in clear, ruby or gold flashed, and milk glass. Jeannette Glass Co. made these in the late 1950s in an opaque Shell Pink. Duncan Miller also made a milk glass version at roughly the same time. Crystal, $15; Crystal with flashing, $25; Milk glass, $30; Shell Pink, $35.

Colony Square, Hazel Ware Division of Continental Can, 1960s. This covered candy is in the very desired "Capri" blue color collected by many glass enthusiasts. Footed with square features, it is quite stunning. Candy Jar with cover. $35.

Moonstone, Hocking Glass Co., 1941-1946. This is a very attractive pattern in crystal with opalescent hobnails and rims creating a bluish effect. Candy dish, handled with cover. $30.

King's Crown, "Thumb Print" line #4016, U. S. Glass Co., 1890s to 1960s. Also made by Indiana Glass Co. in the 1970s. Later pieces made by Indiana tend to be of lesser quality and in a variety of colors popular in the 1970s, such as avocado green. Ruby flashed pieces have been highly desired by collectors for years. Candy Jar, with gold or silver trim, $20; undecorated crystal, $15; with ruby flashed rim, $75.

Canterbury, Duncan Miller, 1938-1955. This is a striking pattern that is normally found in crystal. It has six petal-like edges and a wide bulging optic. Candy Jar, footed in crystal, $45. Desert red, $125.

Manhattan, U.S. Glass Co., Tiffin, and Anchor Hocking. A very attractive pressed pattern that began in the early 1900s and has been made by various companies since then. Candy dish, in beautiful crystal glass with lovely scalloped top edge and thumb print indents on the sides and cover. $15.

Moroccan Swirl, Hazel Ware Division of Continental Can, 1960s. Collected for its color, most collectors simply call it Moroccan Amethyst. The pattern has a distinctive swirled design and very 1960s modern shape. Candy dish with cover, tall, $40; short, $35.

Princess, Indiana Glass Co. A candy dish with a deeply pressed pattern of diamonds and lines. Very popular and available in various colors. Distinctive in appearance. Crystal, $10; colors, $15.

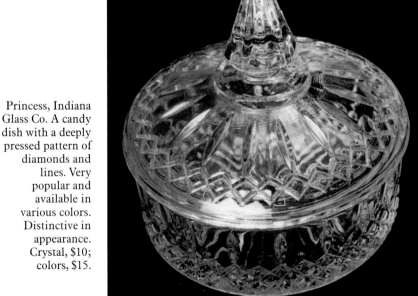

Jubilee, Lancaster
Glass Co., Lancaster,
Ohio. An elegant cut
pattern elaborately
decorated with an
exquisite floral and leaf
design defined by
twelve petal flowers
with open centers. 3-
footed flat bonbon
$50., 3-footed covered
candy $375.

Alexander, line #444, Paden City Glass
Co. Deep ruby red colored covered
candy with ball shaped stem and finial.
This example is etched and gold
encrusted in the Bridal Wreath pattern
but the candy can be found with many
other stunning etchings. $90-$120.

Diamond Point, Indiana Glass
Co., 1950s-1980s. Pattern has a
distinct, four sided diamond
design throughout the glassware
except for a clear band at the
top. Popular covered candy
compotes. Many available
variations of shapes, colors, and
decorations. All types, $15-$20.

Ribbon, Hazel Atlas Glass Corp., 1930-1931. This pattern is recognized by an arrangement of some evenly spaced small panels on certain pieces, while some panels on larger pieces expand in size, giving a flared look. Candy with cover in green. $40.

Fostoria #2380, Confection and Cover. Stunning spiral optic in the cover and base, wide rim, and a bead finial. Made only from 1928-1930 in amber, $35.

Baltimore Pear, Imperial Glass Co. and Jeanette Glass Co. A very attractive covered candy dish with pressed pattern of pears and leaves. Ruby flashed fruits accent the pattern. $25.

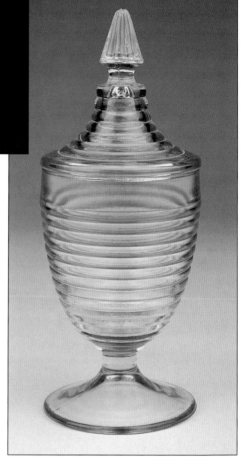

Anchor Hocking Glass Co. Horizontal ringed candy jar with cover. Often referred too as Manhattan, but is simply a go-with piece and not from the true Manhattan line. The rings are rounded on the outside, unlike the pointed ribs of Manhattan. $30-$35.

Right:
Standard Glass Mfg. Co., Lancaster, Ohio. This is Standard's #88 cutting, similar to the Jubilee cutting but with the addition of a swagged lattice pattern on the top edge. This 3-footed candy is currently missing its cover but when complete, $150.

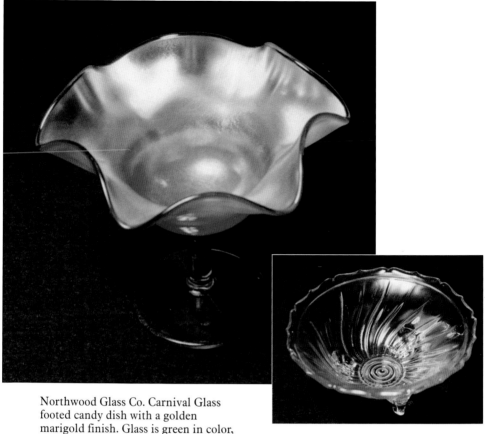

Northwood Glass Co. Carnival Glass footed candy dish with a golden marigold finish. Glass is green in color, which shows through on stem and foot. Simple in form with just a slightly ruffled edge to add appeal. $35-$40.

Swirl or Petal Swirl, Jeanette Glass Co., 1937-1938. Lovely delicate pink swirled pattern candy dish with three small peg legs. The bull's eye pattern in the base and scalloped edge are featured on most of the pieces of this line. $20.

Chapter Eight

Elegance of
the Punch Sets

Punch bowl sets are elegant, useful, and fascinating. Many of the companies produced some very unusual but magnificent sets. One type of complete set consists of 15 pieces: a 1-1/2 gallon punch bowl, twelve 5 oz. punch cups, an 18" punch tray (not in every set), and a ladle.

In other styles, the bowls fit upon an inverted comport or on a specific stand. The bowl can be in a metal holder with an extending flat rim to accommodate cups, as featured in Starlight pattern.

Some salad bowls, the deep 11-1/2" to 12", can be used for a punch bowl. If these are large enough, they can readily serve the purpose—depending upon the number of guests. I have done this and found it to be very convenient and effective. Punch bowls are extremely popular for festive events, such as weddings, anniversaries, graduations, and open house events.

Caribbean, line #112, Duncan Miller Glass Co., 1936-1955. An alluring pattern with continuous wavy or rippled horizontal ribs encircling the outside. When this pattern first appeared it was simply called Wave, for obvious reasons; its name was later changed to Caribbean to give it a more exotic appeal. Punch Bowl, $100; punch plate or under liner, $55; punch cups with applied handles, $12 each.

Norse, Federal Glass Co., later 1960s-1974. A very unique looking punch set with very fine vertical ribbed lines like that of the Homespun pattern. Bottoms of the pieces are plain. Deep bowl upon inverted smaller bowl, cups are plain and un-handled. $30.

Vintage, Anchor Hocking Glass Corporation. A very attractive milk glass set with grapes and leaves on the outside. Gold trim accents the top of this set but it is also seen without. $35.

Fruits, line #2417, Jeanette Glass Company. A classic punch bowl covered with an embossed fruit pattern. Lower parts of the bowl and cups are fluted. Mostly seen in plain crystal but can also be found in cased colors that were produced in the 1970s. A very durable, festive looking set. Punch bowl and cups in crystal, $25; with 1970s cased colors, $45.

Colonial Panel, Pattern #7115, Indiana Glass Co. A majestic punch bowl
set with wide fluted panels on the sides of the bowl and cups. Top edge is
serrated and slightly flared. A thick and brilliant glass of substantial
quality. $75-$100.

Royal Ruby, Anchor Hocking Glass Co., 1939-1960s. A pattern of solid deep red glass that is popular for festive events. Punch bowl and stand, $80; punch cups, $3 each; complete set including twelve cups, $116.

American, line #2056, Fostoria Glass Co., 1915-1987. This is an elegant pattern, consisting of brilliant crystal cubes throughout the glassware. Bowl and short pedestal base. $225.

Starlight, Hazel Atlas Glass Co., 1938-1940. Pattern is made up of a waffle design in the center and crossing over bands of lines on the sides. Reminiscent of a Hollywood movie premier with spotlights shooting into the sky. Punch set, 13" plate, $18; 11-1/2" bowl, $20; cups, $7 each.

Anchor Hocking Glass Co. Simple set with white printed leaves on the bowl and cups. Gold accents on the rims make this set quite delightful. Bowl and twelve cups. $30.

Forest Green, Anchor Hocking, 1950s-1967. Pattern of solid dark green glass that is popular for festive events. Punch bowl, $30; punch bowl base, $50; punch cups, $3 each; complete set with twelve cups, $116.

Mr. B, line #555, Paden City Glass Co. Crystal glass punch set very much in the style of Candlewick. Instead of beads all the same size on the rim, however, it has a larger one every so often mixed in with the smaller ones. Two styles of cups are found, one with teardrops around the bottom and the other plain. $50-$75.

The Concord, "Daisy & Button," Thatcher Manufacturing Co., 1951-1961. Thatcher was a division of McKee Glass Co. and was eventually bought out by Jeanette in 1961. A very fine quality milk glass set with a stars and bars pressed type pattern. Wide flared scalloped rim is quite distinct. Complete set with twelve cups. $55.

Dominion, Smith Glass Co. Cupped edge punch set in
crystal with wide side panels and a diamond pattern on the
lower bottom. Scalloped rim at the top; was not sold with
an under plate. Bowl, $25; plain cups, $4 each.

Tom and Jerry, Hazel Atlas Co., 1940s. A popular opaque white set
decorated in red and green festive holiday colors. Pieces are marked
with the Hazel Atlas logo. Bowl, $25-$30; cups, $3-$4.

Sandwich, Anchor Hocking Glass Co., 1939-1964, 1977. Pattern
has an allover stippling spaced around flowers, foliage, and scroll
motifs in an elaborate arrangement. Punch bowl, $30; punch
bowl stand, $40; cups $4 each; complete 14-piece set, $118.

Vintage, Fostoria Glass Co.,
1904-1929. This is a punch
set with a deep etched
pattern of grapes and leaves
that extends around the
bowl and base. Glass is
blown and is quite brilliant.
Very few of these have
survived. $125-$150.

Chapter Nine

Common Plates Used

The plate, so ordinary, is the essential item in dinnerware sets. Most familiar to us is the 9-1/2" to 10-1/2" dinner plate. This is the one from which we consume most of our food. Some patterns have dinner plates that vary in size. The larger size is more difficult to find.

The luncheon plate, usually 7" to 9", is smaller than a dinner plate and larger than a salad plate. These plates are ideal for lighter meals—small lunches, a light breakfast, or for club meetings. A 7" bread and butter plate is quite common, along with the 7-1/2" salad plate.

The 6" sherbet plate is another small plate; it is so useful and accompanies the sherbet dish.

A complete set can have the dinner, breakfast, luncheon, salad, and bread plates. All of these come in various shapes, such as round, square, oval, hexagonal, and octagonal. Interesting are the shapes of the rims, consisting of scalloped, flared, unflared, cupped edge, rolled edge, serrated, petal shaped, and scroll edged.

Flower Garden with Butterflies, U.S. Glass Co., late 1920s. Plate, 10" blue. $50.

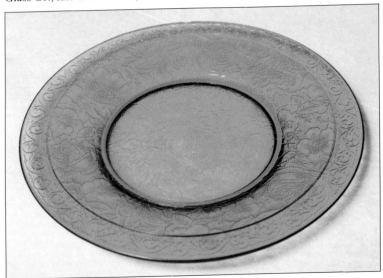

Left: Cremax, 9-3/4" dinner plate, $12.
Right: Vitrock, 10" dinner plate, $12.

Left: Pretzel, 9-1/4" dinner plate, $12. Right:
Waterford "Waffle," 9-1/2" dinner plate, $15.

Left: Royal Lace, 9-3/4" dinner plate, $25.
Right: Ovide, 9" dinner plate, $8.

Left: Swirl "Petal Swirl," 9-1/4" dinner plate, $25.
Right: Old Cafe, 10" dinner plate, $70.

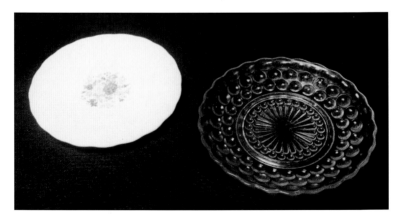

Left: Cremax, 9-3/4" dinner plate, $12.
Right: Bubble, 9-1/4" dinner plate, $10.

Indiana Custard "Flower and Leaf Band," Indiana Glass Co., 1930s. The ivory is a neat pristine pattern made in the early 1930s, consisting of a band of flowers and leaves along each edge. 9-3/4" dinner plate, $33.

Floral "Poinsettia," Jeannette Glass Co., 1931-1935. A beautiful pattern with a floral poinsettia design and vertical panels. 9" pink dinner plate, $22.

Clover Leaf, Hazel Atlas Glass Co., 1930-1936. Lovely pattern of intertwined clovers in a band around the outside and in the center. 8" luncheon plate, $17.

Indiana Custard "Flower and Leaf Band," Indiana Glass Co., 1930s. The ivory is a neat pristine pattern made in the early 1930s consisting of a band of flowers and leaves along each edge. 8-7/8" ivory luncheon plate, $22.

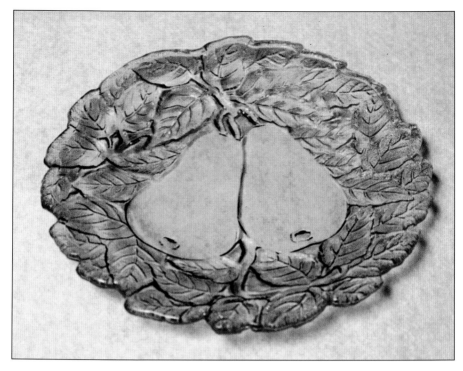

Avocado "Sweet Pear," No.601, Indiana Glass Co., 1923-1933.
A highly desirable pattern consisting of pears in the center
surrounded by a brocade of leaves. 8-1/4" luncheon plate, $25.

Left: Old Colony, 8-1/4" luncheon plate, $30. Right: Colonial "Knife and
Fork," 8-1/2" luncheon plate $13.

Left: "S" Stippled Rose, 8" luncheon plate, $3.
Right: Jubilee, 8-3/4" luncheon plate, $15.

Left: Hobnail, 8-1/2" luncheon plate, $14.
Right: Moonstone, 8-1/4" luncheon plate, $18.

Left: Diamond Quilted, 8" luncheon plate, $12.
Right: Thistle, 8" luncheon plate, $25.

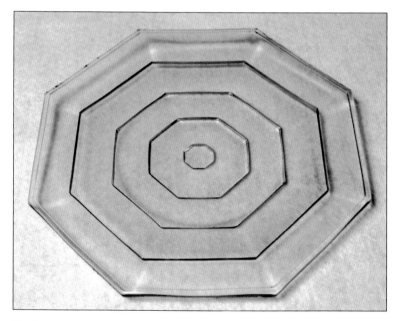

Tea Room, Indiana Glass Co., 1936-1931. 8-1/4" luncheon plate, $35.

Left: American Sweetheart, 8" salad plate, $10.
Right: Laced Edge "Katy Blue," 8" salad plate, $38.

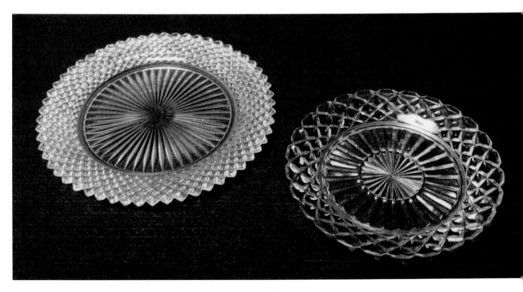

Left: Miss America, 8-1/2" salad plate, $35.
Right: Waterford "Waffle," 8-1/8" salad plate, $8.

Left: Adam, 7-3/4" salad plate, $20. Right: Madrid, 7-1/2" salad plate, $15.

Mt. Pleasant "Double Shield," L.E. Smith Glass Co.,
1920s-1934. Sherbet plate, $12; Sherbet, $15.

Special Thistle, Tiffin Glass Co., 1924-1934.
Under plate, $10; Sherbet, $15.

Jubilee, Lancaster Glass Co., early 1930s. An elegant pattern elaborately
decorated with an exquisite floral and leaf design with twelve petals with
an open center. Sherbet and under plate, $114.

Left: Pretzel, 6" tab handled plate with fruit cup, $10. Right: Waterford "Waffle," 6" sherbet plate and sherbet, $10-$12.

Trojan, Fostoria Glass Co., 1929-1944. Three plates in Topaz: 10-1/4" dinner, $70; 8-3/4" luncheon, $20; 7-1/2" salad, $12.

Chapter Ten

Beauty and Variety
of the Cake Plates

The versatile and attractive cake plates produced back in the 1920s and 30s were extraordinary items. I distinctly remember the pink and green cake plates that my mother received as premium gifts with the purchase of a 25-pound bag of flour. I thought they were the most beautiful pieces of glassware I had ever seen. They were three-footed with the pattern of a stylized sunflower in the center surrounded by a border with quite large flowers and foliage. These are still very popular; collectors love and search for them.

After admiring these cake plates, I began to search for other styles and it was amazing what I found. Cake plates come in a variety of shapes: flat with three legs, tray like, two handled open or closed, the larger type with the groove around the rim for insertion of the lid, and the pedestal type (my favorite), so classic in appearance. They can be used not only for cakes, but also for serving breads, cookies, doughnuts, and other snacks. Surprisingly, some collectors concentrate on cake plates and collect them exclusively. This is great if you have the space.

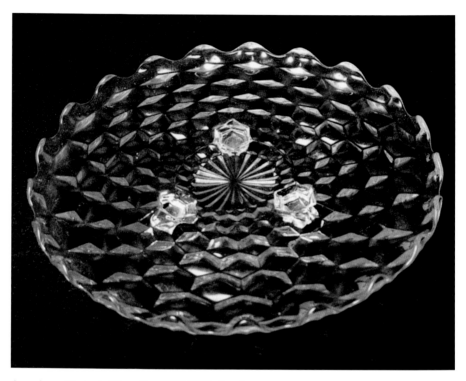

American, Fostoria Glass Co., 1915-1986. An elegant pattern that consists of brilliant crystal cubes throughout the glassware. Cake plate, 12", 3-footed. $35.

Left and right: Sunflower, Jeanette Glass Co., 1930s. This cake plate is one of my favorites. So beautiful with the stylized sunflower in the center surrounded by the border of flowers and foliage. Pink or Green, 10". $25.

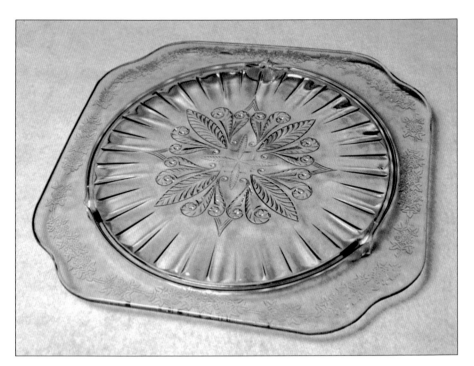

Adam, Jeanette Glass Co., 1932-1934. A beautiful pattern with the center consisting of a group of alternating feathers, plumes, and wide radial ridges and rims. Cake plate, 10" footed. $35.

U.S. Glass, 1924-1960s. Very prolific in the variety of pressed tableware, such as center servers, console sets, and various plates. Cake plate, crystal with a sunburst center, beaded, with a block like rim, scalloped edge and footed. $12 (a premium gift).

Shaggy Daisy, U.S. Glass Co., later 1920s. An early pattern of occasionally found pieces that is very attractive. The center is a daisy surrounded by smaller daisies and scroll like vines. It is 10" wide and found in both pink and green. $25.

Princess, Hocking Glass Co., 1931-1935. Plates are octagonal with a center motif of an eight-spoke snowflake. Rim pattern consists of lines, flowers, and leaves. Cake plate, 10", three legs. $50.

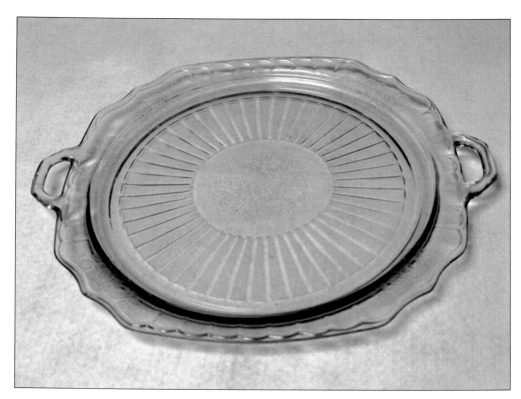

Mayfair "Open Rose," Hocking Glass Co., 1931-1937. A beautiful plate
with a center circle of roses with widely spaced lines, and a border of roses
and scalloped edges. Cake plate, 12", with handles. $70.

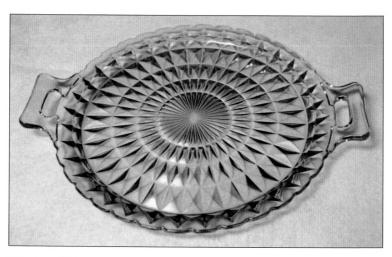

Windsor, "Windsor Diamond," Jeanette Glass Co., 1936-
1946. A pressed pattern resembling cut crystal that consists
of a series of diamond shaped facets emanating from a circle
of radial ribs. Cake plate, pink, 10-3/4", handled, $35.

Sharon, "Cabbage Rose," Federal Glass Co., 1935-1939. A very popular and attractive pattern with a center motif of a curved spray of roses with spokes on the border. Cake plate, 11-1/2" footed. Pink, $50. Crystal, $20.

Anniversary, Jeanette Glass Co., 1947-1949, Late 1960s-1970s.
This pattern has numerous vertical ribs with an open clear space
in the center. Cake plate, 12-1/2", with groove for lid. $9.

Diamond Lattice, U.S. Glass Co., 1920-1930. An early pattern of occasionally found pieces. The plate has a plain center surrounded by a crisscross
design with a block border. Cake plate, 12-3/4", green. $20.

Beauty and Variety of the Cake Plates

Candlewick, Imperial Glass Co., 1936-1984. Elegant
crystal glassware with outstanding or unique beaded
edges. Cake salver, 11-1/4", three ball stem. $140.

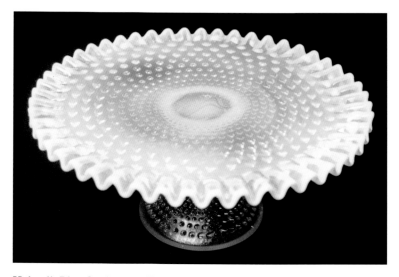

Hobnail, Blue Opalescent, Fenton Art Glass Co., 1940s.
An exquisite pedestal type salver with a crimped edge
and opal hobnails. Footed cake stand, 12". $145.

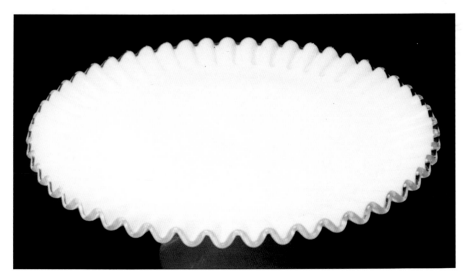

Silver Crest, Fenton Art Glass Co., 1943-present. A very white glassware with a crimped crystal clear edge. Very attractive pattern line that contains countless items to collect. Cake plate, 13" high-footed. $48.

American, line #2056, Fostoria Glass Co., 1915-1981. An elegant pattern that consists of brilliant crystal cubes throughout the glassware. 10" Round pedestal cake stand. $110.

Teardrop, Indiana Glass Co., Dunkirk, Indiana. Simple cake stand with a slight scallop and teardrop pattern spaced out around the edge. $25.

U.S. Glass Co., 1924-1960s. This is an elegant pressed glass cake stand on a pedestal base. Overall pattern consists of various circles, squares, and line. Rounded up edge with a slight scallop. $45.

Candlewick, Imperial Glass Co., 1936-1984. Elegant crystal glassware with outstanding or unique beaded edges. Cake salver, 10", one ball stem. $90.

Spirea Band ("Earl," original company name), Bryce Higbee Co., Pittsburgh, Pennsylvania. This is a very early pressed glass cake stand made around 1890. The pattern around the edge has tiny round eyes inside square boxes. It is quite stunning in the amber color. $75-$100.

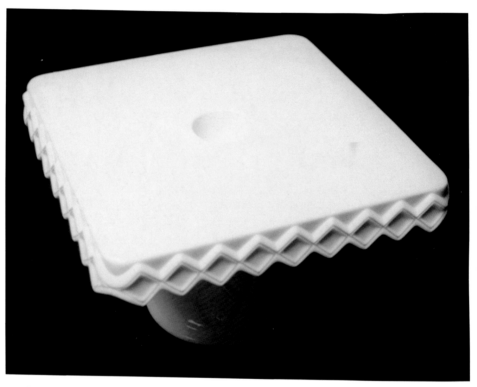

Zigzag, Indiana Glass Co., Dunkirk, Indiana. A very nice attractive solid white square cake stand with an edge design resembling zigzag lines that create squares. $50.

Above and below:

Harp, Jeanette Glass Co., 1954-1957. Harp is a beautiful pattern with a musical name featuring a harp or lyre in a brocaded stipple background, including even the base. Variations in shape and color add interest to collecting this pattern. 9" Cake stand, crystal with gold rim, $25; crystal with ruffled gold rim, $25; ice blue with double combination pattern, $45-$50.

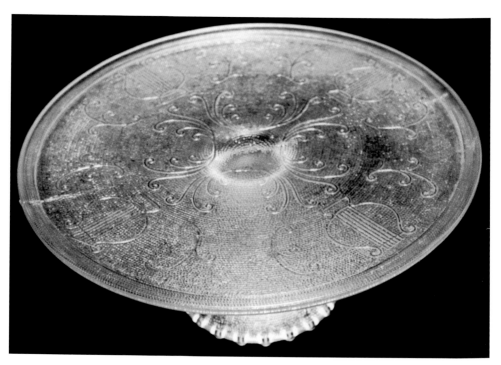

Harp, Jeanette Glass Co., 1954-1957. Another 9"
cake stand, this one crystal with smooth rim, $25.

Trojan, Fostoria Glass Co., 1929-1944. This is a very attractive etched pattern that resembles a spade with additional scrolling around it. Two open handles at the sides create elegance. Handled cake plate, 9-3/4". $65.

Black Forest, Paden City Glass Co., 1920s-1930s. Striking pattern of gold encrusted woodland scene with moose and barking dog. Found in a variety of glass colors, with and without the gold. Black footed cake stand with gold encrusting. $180-$200.

Chapter Eleven

Popularity of Grill
Plates Then and Now

Grill plates, so popular back in the Depression era, might be considered oddities today. They are not really so odd, however, as the modern day divided TV dinner plates or trays are designed for the same purpose.

The grill plate, usually large and divided into three parts, was introduced in the 1930s. Restaurants used them widely. The purpose of these plates was to keep the food separated in the different compartments. They also allowed smaller servings to fill the plate. Today, they can be useful for those who like to eat their food in this manner; some members of my family prefer this type of plate when I serve dinners. I've also given grill plates as gifts and the recipients are fascinated by them.

Grill plates can also be used for serving snacks, like crackers, cheeses, chips, etc., much like a relish dish. Many of the dinner sets included these, so beautifully designed.

Madrid, Federal Glass Co., 1932-1939. This pattern has a scroll like design with some dots and an unusual filigree design. Grill plate, 10-1/2", Amber. $10.

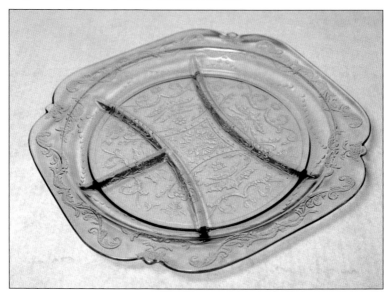

Daisy, No. 620, Indiana Glass Co., 1930s. A pattern with the design of daisies found around the border, giving it its characteristic motif. Crystal grill plate, 10-1/4". $6.

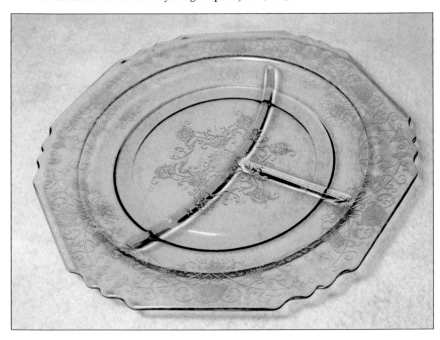

Florentine #1, "Poppy," Hazel Atlas Glass Co., 1932-1935. This pattern has scalloped edges between the straight edges. A center motif of flowers and scrolls in a pinwheel shape is prominent. The borders have elaborate scrolling with flowers resembling poppies. Grill plate, 10", green. $25.

Rose Mary, "Dutch Rose," Federal Glass Co., 1935-1937.
Pattern has a center bouquet of roses placed between an
overlapping looped design. Pink grill plate. $32.

Miss America, Hocking Glass Co., 1935-1938. This is an extremely popular
pattern with its distinctive, easy to recognize sunburst of radial lines and
band of crosshatching on the edge. Grill plate, 10-1/4", Crystal. $12.

U.S. Glass / Tiffin. Green grill plate with a wide, gold encrusted acid etched border. The pattern contains flowers, birds, and scrolls intertwining everything together. $25.

Royal Lace, Hazel Atlas Glass Co., 1934-1941. An outstanding, very decorative and elongated pattern with a motif of lacy scrolls, leaves, and flowers surrounded by a drape design. Grill plate, 9-7/8", Crystal. $12.

Bubble, Anchor Hocking Glass Co., 1940-1965. An easy pattern to recognize with the scalloped edge and radial sunburst center ending in a circle of bull's eye dots. Grill plate, 9-3/8", blue. $25 (rare).

Cloverleaf, Hazel Atlas Glass Co., 1930-1936. The pattern consists of a vine of clovers in the center to create a star. More intertwined clovers create a border around the smooth edge. Grill plate, 10-1/4", green. $30.

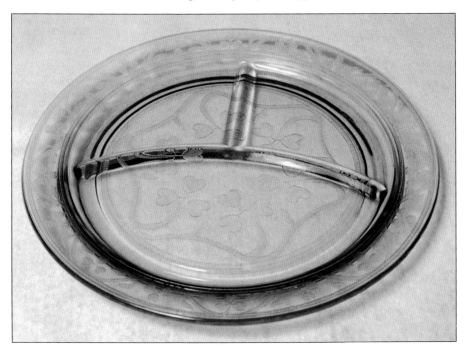

Stippled Band, L.E. Smith. Green grill plate,
simple in form and containing only a stippled
border around the edge for pattern. $12.

Parrot, "Sylvan," Federal Glass Co., 1931-1932. A scenic pattern of
parrots sitting on bamboo branches. Grill plate, 10-1/2", green. $34.

Cameo, "Ballerina," "Dancing Girl," Hocking Glass Co., 1930-1934. This
is the only Depression glass pattern that has a human figure. It features
little dancing girls with long draped scarves appearing in the border,
surrounded by festoons and bows. Grill plate, 10-1/2", green. $20.

Chapter Twelve

The Useful
Sandwich Plates

Sandwich plates are large—they can be 12" to 15-1/2" in diameter. Some of them can be called chop plates, torte plates, or tray servers with handles.

A salver, a round tray or platter on a high stem, is also attractive and useful for serving tea sandwiches and desserts.

Several patterns in the elegant patterns have more than one torte plate, quite large and very elegant with the curved in rim. These plates are also featured with the large bowls (salad) and make beautiful sets. In one pattern, the sandwich plate is featured with a metal handle.

All of these plates are extremely useful, especially when serving buffet style.

Candlewick, Imperial Glass Co., 1936-1984. Elegant crystal glassware with outstanding and unique beaded edges. Handled plate, 8", Crystal. $30.

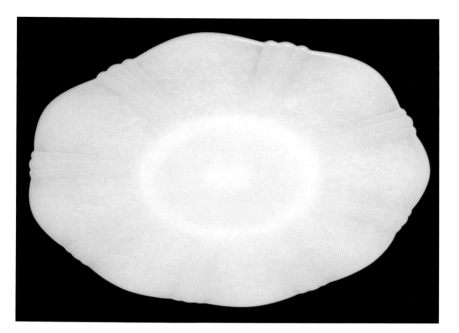

American Sweetheart, MacBeth-Evans Glass Co., 1931-1936. This is a delicate pattern with a neat arrangement consisting of a center motif of festoons, ribbons, and scrolls with smaller ones surrounding the scalloped rim with short lines. 12" Salver in Monax $35; pink, $30.

Open Work, "Laced Edge," Lancaster Glass Co., early 1930s. Many pieces were also produced in pink and green with hand decorated and satin finishes. Topaz frosted 12-1/2" sandwich plate. $20.

Lido, Fostoria Glass Co., 1937-1960. This is Fostoria's #329
etching of palm trees on the Baroque blanks. Glass is of
excellent quality and brilliance. Torte plate, 14", Crystal. $50.

Star, Federal Glass Co., Late 1950s and early 1960s. This pattern has a
striking star with an outburst of rays. Sandwich plate, 11-3/4", yellow. $12.

Laurel, Indiana Glass Co., 1950s-1960s. A lovely pattern
that reflects great amounts of light. Star pattern in the
center with a laurel leaf border on the outer rim. $25.

Horseshoe #612, Indiana Glass Co., 1930-1933. This pattern, especially the
plate, is entirely decorated in one uninterrupted design of elaborate scroll
forming a snowflake like pattern. Sandwich plate, 11-1/2", green. $28.

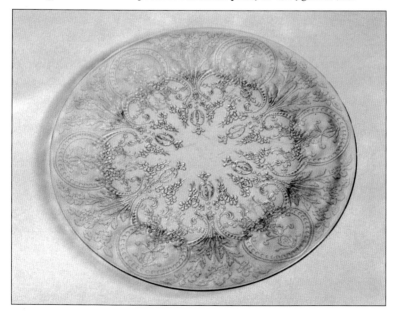

Camellia, Jeanette Glass Co., 1950s. An attractive pattern in crystal with a camellia flower design in the bottom of some pieces or in the center. Clear 12" sandwich plate. $14.

Cherry Blossom, Jeanette Glass Co., 1930-1939. A true depression mold, consisting of an etched pattern in an opaque glass color with a profuse allover pattern. Handled sandwich tray, 10-1/2", green. $45.

Harp, Jeannette Glass Co., 1954-1957 A very beautiful pattern with a
musical name featuring a harp or lyre in a dainty allover beading, even on
the bottom. Service tray with open handles, 10" x 15-1/2", Crystal. $40.

Lancaster Glass Co., Jubilee cut pattern of the early 1930s. An
elegant cut pattern elaborately decorated with an exquisite floral
and leaf design defined by twelve petal flowers with open
centers. Three-footed sandwich plate, 13-1/2", Topaz. $200.

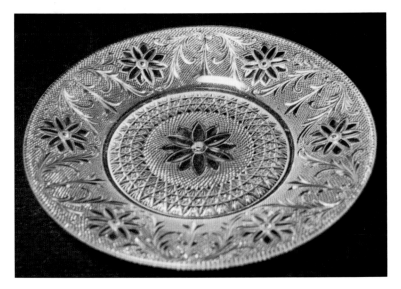

Sandwich, Indiana Glass Co., 1920s-1980s. This pattern
has an allover stippling spaced around flowers, foliage,
and scroll motifs. Plate, 13", Crystal. $14.

Petalware, MacBeth-Evans Glass Company. A very popular pattern
with a center design of concentric circles surrounded by a wide band
of plain glass and a circle inside the scalloped rim. Pink salver. $20.

Cremax, MacBeth-Evans Division of Corning Glass Works, late 1930s and early 1940s. This pattern with the pink piecrust edging and a solid center is becoming very popular. Sandwich plate, 12". $15.

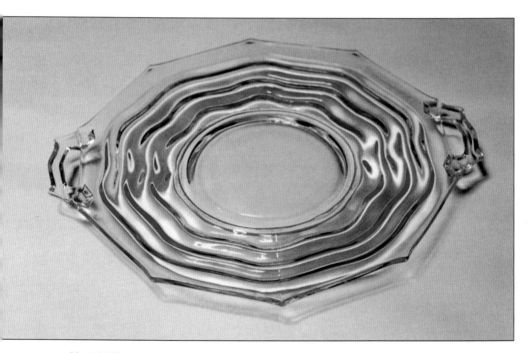

No. 190 Tearoom or Fountain line, Jenkins Glass Co., late 1920s and early 1930s. This is a pattern that resembles waves or ripples in the water. A full table service was made and can be collected. Service plate with open handles, 10-1/2", green. $30.

Manhattan, "Horizontal Ribbed," Anchor Hocking Glass Co., 1939-1941. Pattern is easily recognized with its wide shape and ribbed design. Sandwich plate, 14", Crystal. $28.

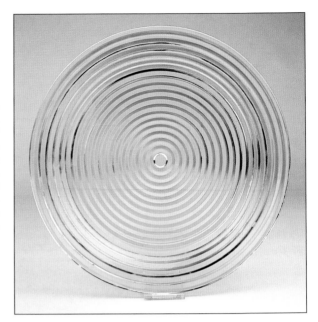

Lorain Basket, line #615, Indiana Glass Co., 1929-1932. An attractive pattern that contains conventional baskets of flowers and a center of scrolls and garlands surrounded by an 8-sided swag ending in finials and scrolls. Serving tray or platter, 11-1/2", yellow. $48.

Pretzel, Indiana Glass co., late 1930s-1980s. A unique intertwined pretzel type pattern scrolled around the edges. Sandwich plate, 11-1/2", Crystal. $15 (no center design).

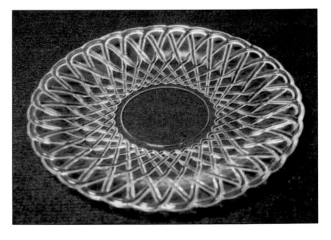

Tyrus, cutting #28, Standard Glass Mfg. Co., Lancaster, Ohio. Large flared tray with a braided cable border around the base foot. The cutting is very much like Jubilee with the same type of open flower. $120.

Heritage, Federal Glass Co., 1940-1955. A striking pattern in crystal with a flower design in a petal and an extensive beaded background. Sandwich plate, 12", Crystal. $16.

Cambridge Glass Co., 1930s. This is the Cambridge #214
tab handled serving tray used for many purposes. Raised
edge and a star bottom pattern. Crystal 10" tray. $35.

Indiana Glass Co., 1950s and 1960s. This is a heavy sandwich tray with a
thumbprint pattern fanned on the outside edge and a diamond type design
on the inner edge. It is Indiana's line #1007. Sandwich tray, 10", Crystal. $30.

Chapter Thirteen

A Complete Dinnerware Set

Lake Como, Anchor Hocking Glass Co., 1935-1937. A dinnerware set of a delphinium blue decoration on Vitrock white dinnerware.

Aurora, Hazel Atlas Glass Co., in the late 30s. Setting in cobalt blue.

Manhattan, "Horizontal Ribbed," Anchor
Hocking Glass Co., 1939-1941. Setting in crystal.

Cremax, MacBeth-Evans Division of Corning
Glass Works, late 1930s and early 1940s.
Ivory decorated setting.

Chapter Fourteen

Summary of
Dinnerware Sets

The table settings of the 1920s and 30s were something to be admired. The style of setting the table in one design and one color with a variety of accessories will always be remembered. Every piece served a purpose for the family meal. This was truly the era of gracious living but, sadly, in our fast paced and complex society this manner of living seems to have vanished. I hope that by featuring the variety of accessories shown here, this book can help to bring back the nostalgic charm of this style once again.

It is still possible today to assemble and use a full dinner service of the 1920s-60s. The search is fun and the cost can be less than buying a new set.

Dinner setting, Madrid, Federal Glass Co., 1932-1939.

Dinner setting, Star, Federal Glass Co., 1950s.

Dinner setting, "Bubble," Fire King, Hocking Glass Co., 1941-1965.

Dinner setting, "S" pattern, "Stippled Rose
Band," MacBeth-Evans Glass Co., 1934-1935.

Dinner setting, Sierra, "Pinwheel," Jeanette Glass Co., 1931-1933.

Dinner setting, Waterford, "Waffle," Hocking Glass Co., 1938-1944.

Luncheon setting, Cloverleaf, Hazel Atlas Glass Co., 1930-1936.

Luncheon setting, Diamond Quilted, "Flat Diamond,"
Imperial Glass Co., 1920s-1930s.

Luncheon setting, Horseshoe #612, Indiana Glass Co., 1930-1933.

Luncheon setting, Tea Room, Indiana Glass Co., 1926-1931.

Bibliography

Florence, Gene. *Collectible Glassware From the 40s 50s 60s*. Paducah, KY: Collector Books, 2002.

Florence, Gene. *Collector's Encyclopedia of Depression Glass*. Paducah, KY: Collector Books, 2002.

Florence, Gene. *Elegant Glassware of the Depression Era*. Paducah, KY: Collector Books, 2001.

Kovel, Ralph and Terry. *Kovels Depression Glass & American Dinnerware*. New York, NY: Crown Publishers, Inc., 1991

Mauzy, Jim and Barbara. *Mauzy's Comprehensive Handbook of Depression Glass 4th Edition*. Atglen, PA: Schiffer Publishing, Ltd., 2002.

Yeske, Doris. *Depression Glass & Beyond*. Atglen, PA: Schiffer Publishing, Ltd., 2003.

Yeske, Doris. *Depression Glass, a Collector's Guide 6th Edition*. Atglen, PA: Schiffer Publishing, Ltd., 2003.

Yeske, Doris. *Depression Glass: Collections & Reflections*. Atglen, PA: Schiffer Publishing, Ltd., 2002.